FESTIVALS and CELEBRATIONS

Diwali

By Louise Nelson

KidHaven PUBLISHING

Published in 2023 by
KidHaven Publishing, an Imprint of Greenhaven Publishing, LLC
2544 Clinton St., Buffalo, NY 14224

Written by: Louise Nelson
Edited by: William Anthony
Designed by: Amy Li
Image Credits: All images are courtesy of Shutterstock.com. With thanks to Getty Images, Thinkstock Photo and iStockphoto.
Recurring images – TinyDoz (character), krishnasomya (pattern), svetichstock, Auspicious, littleWhale, girafchik (vectors). 4–5 – Irina Thalhammer, Milton Buzon. 6–7 – Art Alex, Random Illustrator, PRASANNAPIX, StockImageFactory.com. 8–9 – Anant Jadhav, StockImageFactory.com. 10–11 – Lukasz Szwaj, snapgalleria, stockshoppe. 12–13 – Abie Davies, StockImageFactory.com. 14–15– AALA IMAGES, StockImageFactory.com, wavebreakmedia. 16–17 – Din Mohd Yaman, Reshma Pradhan14. 18–19 – Wei Huang, StockImageFactory.com. 20–21 – highviews, sdx15. 22–23 – Lukasz Szwaj, Creative Hatti, Mariusz S. Jurgielewicz.

Cataloging-in-Publication Data

Names: Nelson, Louise.
Title: Diwali / Louise Nelson.
Description: New York : KidHaven Publishing, 2023. | Series: Festivals and celebrations | Includes glossary and index.
Identifiers: ISBN 9781534543140 (pbk.) | ISBN 9781534543164 (library bound) | ISBN 9781534543171 (ebook)
Subjects: LCSH: Divali--Juvenile literature. | Fasts and feasts--Hinduism--Juvenile literature.
Classification: LCC BL1239.82.D58 N45 2023 | DDC 294.5'36--dc23

Manufactured in the United States of America

CPSIA compliance information: Batch #CWKH23: For further information contact Greenhaven Publishing LLC at 1-844-317-7404.

Please visit our website, www.greenhavenpublishing.com.
For a free color catalog of all our high-quality books, call toll free 1-844-317-7404 or fax 1-844-317-7405.

Find us on

Contents

Words that look like this can be found in the glossary on page 24.

What Is a Festival?

A festival is when people come together to celebrate something special or an important time of year. Some festivals are celebrated with a feast or a parade.

Festivals are a good time to get together with your community to celebrate.

Sometimes, a festival might be part of a religion. Diwali is a big festival that is celebrated by Hindus, Sikhs, and Jains around the world. It means something different to different religions.

In this book, we will look at how Hindus celebrate Diwali.

Hinduism

Hinduism is the religion that Hindus follow. It is thought that Hinduism began in India over 4,000 years ago.

Hindus believe in many gods and goddesses.

Ganesh

Lord Ganesh is known as the god of new beginnings and wisdom, and people pray to him at the beginning of things.

Lakshmi

Lakshmi is known as the goddess of wealth and good fortune.

Diwali

Diwali is the festival of lights. It is a bright, colorful, and happy time. People celebrate Diwali between October and November, but the date changes every year.

The word Diwali means "row of lights."

Hindus celebrate the Hindu New Year during Diwali. The festival can last for five days. It is a fun time for family and friends to spend together.

Shubh Diwali means "Happy Diwali" in Hindi.

The Story

Different people think about different stories during Diwali. One of these stories is about Rama and Sita.

There was once a prince called Rama and a princess called Sita. An evil king called Ravana wanted to make Sita his wife, so he kidnapped her.

When Rama found out, he was very upset. He asked the monkey god Hanuman to help him find Princess Sita.

Hanuman found Sita imprisoned on an island. He got his monkey army ready to fight Ravana and free Sita.

It was a big battle and it lasted for a long time. Finally, Rama shot Ravana with a magical golden arrow, which hit him in the chest. Sita was saved!

It was time for Rama and Sita to go back home, but it was very dark. The villagers lit lamps to help them find their way back.

This is why people light lamps during Diwali.

Diyas

Diyas are the lamps that people light for Diwali. They are very important because they remind many people of the story of Rama and Sita.

Diwali is a time to celebrate good triumphing over evil.

Hindus honor the goddess Lakshmi during Diwali. The lights and lamps help Lakshmi find her way to people's homes and bring them good fortune in the new year.

Sparklers and fireworks are another fun way to celebrate Diwali.

Getting Ready

It is very important to have clean homes during Diwali. Many people clean, tidy, and redecorate so their homes are ready for when Lakshmi visits.

Before Diwali, many people go shopping for new clothes. This is so they can wear new clothes on each day of Diwali.

Girls may wear lehengas and boys may wear kurtas.

Rangoli

Rangoli are beautiful patterns. They are made from colorful chalk, rice powder, and pastes. They can sometimes look like flowers.

People draw rangoli on the floor outside their homes to welcome guests, including Lakshmi, and bring good luck. Some rangoli patterns are so small that they can fit on a doorstep. Others are much bigger.

At the Mandir

It is common to worship Lord Ganesh and the goddess Lakshmi during Diwali. Many Hindus visit mandirs to pray to them and leave them offerings.

Mandirs are Hindu temples. This is the BAPS Shri Swaminarayan Mandir in London.

At the mandir, Hindus make offerings to Ganesh and Lakshmi. These might be flowers, lit diyas, sweets, and other types of food. They are usually given on a special plate called puja thali.

This puja thali set is ready for Diwali.

Food

During Diwali, different people eat different foods. Some people eat Indian sweets called mithai. One type of Indian sweet is called barfi.

Barfi is pronounced "bur-fee."

Hindus offer mithai to the gods. Some people also like to give their friends and family boxes of mithai during Diwali.

Diwali Around the World

Diwali is celebrated by people all around the world. From Fiji to Singapore, Malaysia to Australia, each country has its own way of celebrating Diwali.

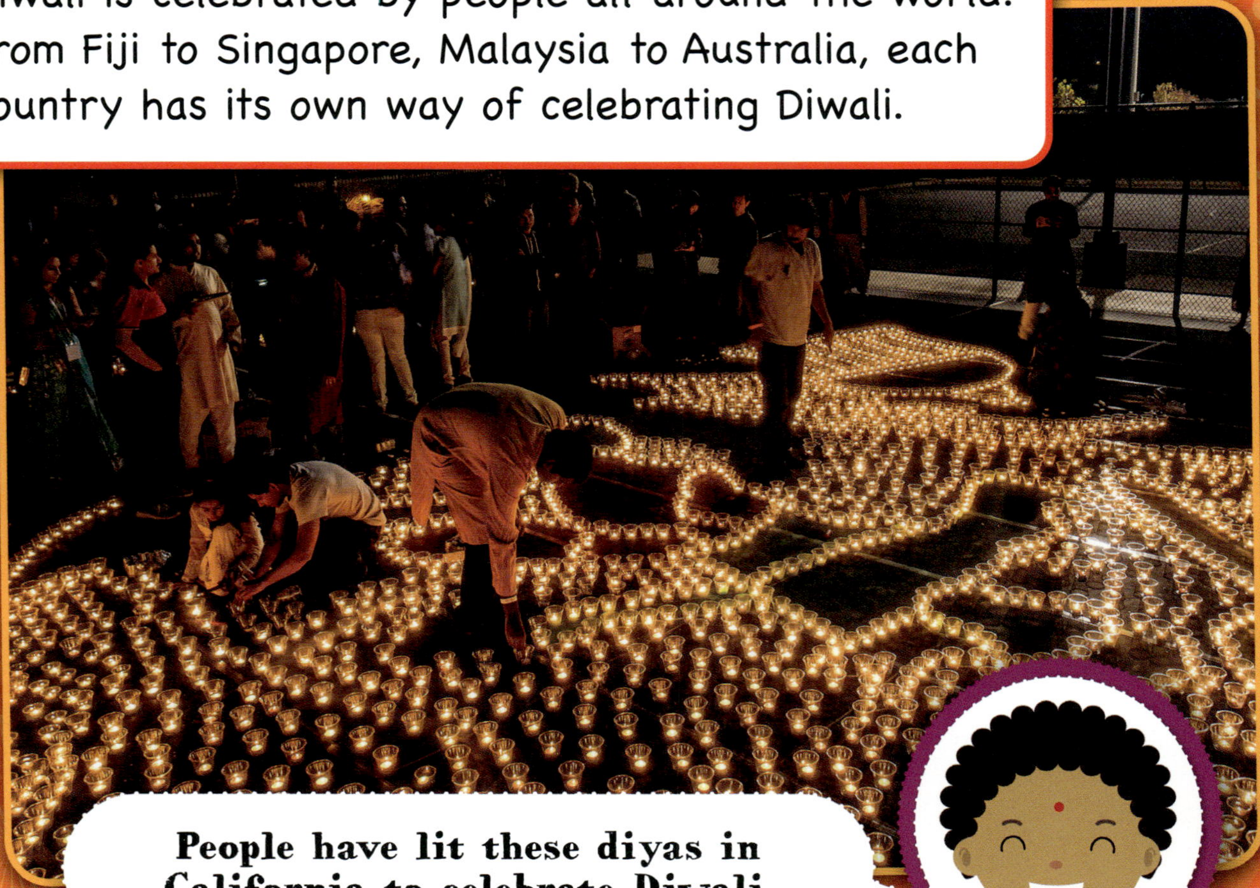

People have lit these diyas in California to celebrate Diwali.

Quiz

What have you learned about Diwali?

1. Who celebrates Diwali?

2. Who is the goddess of wealth and good fortune?

3. What is the name of the monkey god from the Diwali story?

4. What are rangoli patterns made from?

5. Can you name a type of mithai?

Answers: 1. Hindus, Sik'hs and Jains, 2. Lakshmi, 3. Hanuman, 4. Colorful chalk, rice powder, and pastes, 5. Barfi

Glossary

community	a group of people who are connected by something
fortune	luck
honor	when lots of people have respect for a person or god and their actions
imprisoned	locked up or held somewhere as a prisoner
Jains	believers in Jainism, a very old Indian religion whose followers do not believe in any gods
parade	when people walk or dance down a street with others watching
religion	a set of beliefs about how the world was made and how a person should live their life that a group of people follow
Sikhs	members of Sikhism, a religion founded around 500 years ago in South Asia, whose followers believe in one God
triumphing	winning in a great victory or success
wealth	a large amount of something, usually money
wisdom	good knowledge, judgement, or understanding of something
worship	a religious act where a person shows their love for a god

Index